It's Q!

Katherine Hengel

Consulting Editor, Diane Craig, M.A./Reading Specialist

Published by ABDO Publishing Company, 8000 West 78th Street, Edina, Minnesota 55439. Copyright © 2010 by Abdo Consulting Group, Inc. International copyrights reserved in all countries. No part of this book may be reproduced in any form without written permission from the publisher. Super SandCastle™ is a trademark and logo of ABDO Publishing Company.

Printed in the United States.

 PRINTED ON RECYCLED PAPER

Editor: Liz Salzmann
Content Developer: Nancy Tuminelly
Cover and Interior Design and Production: Kelly Doudna, Mighty Media
Photo Credits: Corbis Images, iStockphoto (Jani Bryson, Laure Neish, George Peters, Kevin Thomas), Shutterstock

Library of Congress Cataloging-in-Publication Data

Hengel, Katherine.
  It's Q! / Katherine Hengel.
       p. cm. -- (It's the alphabet!)
  ISBN 978-1-60453-604-1
  1. English language--Alphabet--Juvenile literature. 2. Alphabet books--Juvenile literature. I. Title.
  PE1155.H4682 2010
  421'.1--dc22
  〈E〉
                                        2009022027

Super SandCastle™ books are created by a team of professional educators, reading specialists, and content developers around five essential components—phonemic awareness, phonics, vocabulary, text comprehension, and fluency—to assist young readers as they develop reading skills and strategies and increase their general knowledge. All books are written, reviewed, and leveled for guided reading, early reading intervention, and Accelerated Reader® programs for use in shared, guided, and independent reading and writing activities to support a balanced approach to literacy instruction.

About SUPER SANDCASTLE™

**Bigger Books for Emerging Readers
Grades K–4**

Created for library, classroom, and at-home use, Super SandCastle™ books support and engage young readers as they develop and build literacy skills and will increase their general knowledge about the world around them. Super SandCastle™ books are an extension of SandCastle™, the leading preK–3 imprint for emerging and beginning readers. Super SandCastle™ features a larger trim size for more reading fun.

Let Us Know
Super SandCastle™ would like to hear your stories about reading this book. What was your favorite page? Was there something hard that you needed help with? Share the ups and downs of learning to read. We want to hear from you! Send us an e-mail.

sandcastle@abdopublishing.com

Contact us for a complete list of SandCastle™, Super SandCastle™, and other nonfiction and fiction titles from ABDO Publishing Company.

www.abdopublishing.com • 8000 West 78th Street
Edina, MN 55439 • 800-800-1312 • 952-831-1632 fax

Aa Bb Cc Dd Ee
Ff Gg Hh Ii Jj Kk
Ll Mm Nn Oo Pp
Qq Rr Ss Tt Uu Vv
Ww Xx Yy Zz

The Letter Qq

Q and q can also look like

Qq **Qq** Qq Qq Qq Qq

The letter q is
a consonant.

It is the 17th
letter of the
alphabet.

Some words start with **q**.

quail

quilt

6

queen

The letter q almost always has the letter u after it.

The queen quickly covers the quiet quail with a quilt.

Some words have **q** in the middle.

aquarium

liquids

banquet

Joaquin drinks liquids at a banquet in an aquarium.

Joaquin

qu as in bou**qu**et

bouqu**et**

sequ**oia**

Monique

Monique climbs a sequoia carrying a bouquet.

11

squ as in **squ**are

squid

squash

squirrel

The squirrel shares a square squash with a squid.

14

Queen Jacquie is going
to Quebec on a quest.

She brings her duck Quinn
because he is the best.

Jacquie and Quinn are on a quest for something rare.

They are looking for a quilt that is perfectly square!

Queen Jacquie packs a squash and a couple of quarters.

Then she takes a quick question from one of her supporters.

We ♥ Queen Jacquie!

"How will you find this quilt?"
asks Quiggley the quail.

"I'm not quite sure," says the queen.
"Quilts do not leave a trail!"

It's cold in Quebec, but Jacquie and Quinn do not quit.

"When we find it," says Jacquie, "we'll have a banquet!"

Quack!

The quest is quite quiet,
but then Quinn starts to quack.

"I see a square quilt," quacks Quinn.
"It's hanging by that shack!"

Which words have
the letter **q**?

ticket

bouquet

squash

squirrel

ladybug

quarter

rooster

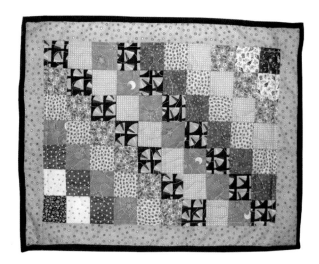

quilt

23

Glossary

banquet (pp. 9, 19) – a large dinner for many people held to celebrate something.

bouquet (pp. 10, 11, 22) – a bunch of flowers gathered together or arranged in a vase.

couple (p. 17) – about two of something.

quilt (pp. 6, 7, 16, 18, 20, 23) – a blanket with two layers of cloth sewn around a warm filling such as wool or cotton.

rare (p. 16) – uncommon.

sequoia (pp. 10, 11) – a kind of very large evergreen tree.

shack (p. 20) – a small cabin or hut.

squid (pp. 12, 13) – a sea animal with a soft body and ten tentacles around the mouth.

supporter (p. 17) – someone who helps someone or is in favor of something.

To promote letter recognition, letters are highlighted instead of glossary words in this series. The page numbers above indicate where the glossary words can be found.

More Words with Q

Find the **q** in the beginning or middle of each word.

acquire	headquarters	quantity	quiver	squawk
conquer	inquire	quarrel	quiz	squeak
consequence	mosquito	quart	quote	squeeze
equal	quake	quarterback	raquet	squire
equator	qualify	queer	request	squirm
frequent	quality	quicksand	require	squirt

MATH QUIZ   Name:

4 + 6 = 10

3 + 2 = 5

14 + 5 =

15

= 15

3 = 8